Sky Furniture

Sky Furniture

Poems by

Ina Anderson

© 2024 Ina Anderson. All rights reserved.
This material may not be reproduced in any form, published,
reprinted, recorded, performed, broadcast,
rewritten, or redistributed without
the explicit permission of Ina Anderson.
All such actions are strictly prohibited by law.

Cover design by Shay Culligan
Cover image by Neil Bartlett
Author photo by Peter Anderson

ISBN: 978-1-63980-644-7

Kelsay Books
502 South 1040 East, A-119
American Fork, Utah 84003
Kelsaybooks.com

For Peter,
always

Acknowledgments

Grateful thanks to the editors of the following publications in which poems in this book first appeared, sometimes in earlier versions:

The Herald of Randolph: "Sky Furniture," "Catastrophic," "To My Great-Granddaughter Not Yet Born"
Literary North: "Cloud Speaks"
The Mountain Troubadour: "Border," "After Harvesting Ramps from the Vermont Woods in Early May," "Catastrophic"
The Party Cabinet: "To Find the Hedgehog," "Arrival," "On the Hill," "Bad Off"
Perhaps It Was the Pie: "Varanasi"
Poem Town Randolph: "My Mother's Bag," "The Taj Across the River," "Concert," "Thank You for Your Service," "Invasion," "Sky Furniture," "Catastrophic"

My heartfelt thanks to teachers past and present who made of me a poet: Curly Whittle, Carolyn Forche, Eileen Myles, Peter Money, Mark Doty, Cynthia Huntington, Major Jackson, Baron Wormser, Verandah Porche.

My gratitude and love to my fellow members of the Pie Poets, together now for over thirteen years: Doreen Spencer Ballard, Beverly Breen, Debby Franzoni, Marjorie Nelson Matthews, Hatsy McGraw.

Contents

I: Back

To Meet the Hedgehog	15
Suds	17
The Peaches	18
Truth	19
Forever	21
My Mother's Bag	23
Dad's Bow Tie	24
Arrival	25
Basket	26
The Apron	27
On the Hill	30

II: Far

At Istanbul Airport	33
Karacaagac	34
The Taj Across the River	36
At the Carpet Factory	37
Varanasi	38
Rajasthan	40

III: Them

Concert	43
Sunny Acres	44
Bad Off	45
PTSD	47
Thank You for Your Service	49
To Take the Dead Weight	50

IV: Other

Border	53
Invasion	54
This I Pray	55
Plight	56
Why I Stole His Lamp	57
Another Color	58

V: Outside

At Zero	61
Field Notes from Jane's Farm, Kirkby Lonsdale	62
Along the Edge	63
Trick of the Light	64
April	65
After Harvesting Ramps in the Vermont Woods in Early May	66
Nasturtiums	68
This I Pray	69
Cloud Speaks	70
Sky Furniture	71
Fell Dreams	72
Geese	73
Trees	75

VI: Soon

Granddaughter	79
Unnoticed	80
Refuge	81

Jane's Farm, Cumbria, 2019	82
When We Are Gone	84
To My Great-Granddaughter Not Yet Born	85

VII: Late

Born	89
By the Side of the Road	90
Off Ramp	91
Enough	92
Catastrophic	93

I: Back

To Meet the Hedgehog

When I rode Stan's little Shetland stallion,
I always found the hedgehog.
I came to expect it.
But lots of other things had to be in place.
Stan's petrol tins lined up neatly along his wall.
His wife serving tripe in the blue dish, not the gold.

So the night the poacher came to my house,
live salmon gasping in his wellies, eyes bulging
in supplication for bubbling, gurgling mercy,
I was wary of paying out the customary five shillings
from my mother's purse, wary I'd break the cantrip,
spoil the magic, and never meet my prickly friend again.
No sniffling, no sharing breath, never a chance
to lie down nose-to-nose, even for just a moment,
joining in its world of insects, and squigglers,
and occasional milk.

It was Stan's suggestion that saved me.
Stan, as he hacked again and again at the stump
of an apple tree by the hen house to make way
for the new white pony, son of his stallion.
Stan, who always gave away an old petrol tin
if he acquired a new one, so the line
along his wall didn't get rumply.
Stan, who brought his cloth cap
to my mother to mend for him,
regularly every autumn.

Child, he said to me, bring it kitten treats.
They have them at the Post Office.
It can't resist them and
it'll eat them out of your hand.

My pocket money was just enough.
That night I lay in the damp grass
nose-to-nose again with the hedgehog.

Suds

Mum thought I should do it,
and probably she was right.
Barely ten, with a
stool under my feet,
every night I washed the dishes.

There was only mum and dad and me,
not many plates and glasses,
but mum was such a cook
and her pans needed a good scrub.
I sighed and began.

There was a big dark window behind the sink,
the flower pots on the old wall.
There was my reflection!
I could see me scrubbing in those suds,
just like a grown-up.
I looked like I was on the telly!

And so each night I put on a show.
Hands busy in the soapy water,
I'd tell my version of the Evening News.
How Queen Elizabeth would have
seventeen children.
How Prince Charles would
climb Everest on a motorbike.
How the nuns at my school deserved
new knickers 'cos the ones I'd
seen on their washing line were
almost in shreds.

And once the pots and pans
were sparkling clean
in those Fairy Liquid suds,
then wiped all neat and dry,
I'd end my TV show and say Goodnight.

The Peaches

Time to stop said my dad
as he pulled our grey Singer
under the trees in the cobbled
yard of an old auberge.
Time to stop for the night,
to walk, run, feel the late light
after a long-driving day.
Old lace curtains shifted, a face
moved across the glass.
With a creak the door stirred,
a sturdy woman in dusty black,
an apron, hair in a gentle bun,
arm laden with an old basket.
As we pulled ourselves from the car,
she drew out three pink-golden orbs,
velvet, wafting sweet.
Bonjour, monsieur, madame, mademoiselle,
voulez-vous une peche?
Et voulez-vous une chambre?
Ah, oui, we chorused,
Oui, une peche!
Et, oui, une chambre.
Dazzled, I sank my young
teeth into the heavenly flesh,
juice exploding down my chin.

Truth

No, damn you, it's true.
I don't care what you say.
She was out there in the garden,
most nights she was out there,
certainly always when the moon was full.
She moved with the breeze,
ran with the wind,
raced into the storms.

And, yes, many times
I joined her, held her hand.
Rough it was,
not quite cold but never warm.
She led me carefully, wary for my feet.
Not like hers, mine
were tender useless things.

And when we reached the big stones,
she put her arms around me.
Carefully now, she drew me to her,
only then began her song.

Isis, Astarte, Diana, Hecate,
Dimitri, Kali, Inanna

And on the third verse
she whispered me to join with her,
to learn her songs, the important songs
I've known now all my life.
She made sure of that.

Yes, mother, you have forgotten.
You have chosen to forget.
You trusted in other powers,
held on to artificial light,
artificial tears.

Do not deny me this.
I know it to be true.
I see it every time
I pass the mirror.

Forever

Back when I believed in the Virgin Mary,
that she was Queen of Heaven and all that,
that she had a really cute halo,
and her favorite color was blue,
back then I believed in a lot of things.

I believed that the tide would always
come up the estuary well past Foxfield,
and that my uncle Jimmy's taxi would never crash.
I believed Queen Elizabeth would live forever
and was probably the Virgin Mary's sister.
I believed my parents would live forever, too.

It wasn't that mum didn't warn me.
"Everyone dies," she said, but I didn't believe her.
Me, I was going on forever, and they'd
come along with me, even to the stars and back.

My dad liked adventures, and he had me liking them too.
We'd find secret stone circles,
been there thousands of years,
and we always got out of there safely
and found a good place to eat our sandwiches.
He drove us fast in his Singer Sports
and we always came out in one piece.
I knew we always would.

So when they both went and died on me,
to say I was completely thrown to my knees
would be an understatement.
It was dark, dark, dark,
and I believed I was going there too.
And it lasted a long, long time.
Surely I'd see them again? Surely!

And this is what keeps me up at night.
This is what keeps me awake and ready.
They're coming!
They're coming!
I know they are.
I know they are.

My Mother's Bag

It was a private kind of bag, the sort
you would not trespass in, the sort
that kept small secrets,
little reparations for slight accidents and upsets,
small repairs and personal adjustments.

There was so much pink in there,
lipstick and rouge, a small box
of pills in a bright fuchsia wrapper,
spare knickers squashed into a bundle,
held by a rubber band.

And always there were dog treats in an old snuff tin,
carried just in case a friend's pup
might snuffle her knees,
look at her with pleading eyes,
memories of her long-lost Tinker.

And a slim secret notebook, soft leather bound,
notes she'd take when visited by inspiration,
visions she'd see and later on commit to oils,
pictures she'd hide in the attic, revealed
only after she was gone, too late
to tell her how we were in awe.

Dad's Bow Tie

You don't have to tie it,
it's on a clip,
a quick-get-away tie,
a bow made ready for a hurry.
Black with tiny dots of white,
it's silky to my fingers.
The shape is neat, it's small,
it's no way flashy.

Most days my dad would wear
a tie skillfully knotted, efficiently draped.
A jacket always, and a smile.
This bow tie, though, would offer him a change.
Perhaps it put a spring in his step
or took the pressure off a rush.

I'm older now than when my father died,
yet decades have not faded my gratefulness.
Where other women learned to yield,
to shave their dreams, to think just small,
my father always let me know my worth.
"Our Ina's a grand lass, clever, she's going far.
'Twas a daughter I wanted.
Been a boy, I'd've sent him back!"

Arrival

When they called out
"English,"
"English,"
"English,"
at the coffee counter at JFK airport
at 5 o'clock in the USA morning
after a night flight from London,
me, first time here,
a wide-eyed innocent,
and all they meant was English muffin,
something that doesn't exist,
and every time they called it out,
I jumped,
I jumped,
I jumped.

Basket

It's willow, this basket,
squared off and sturdy,
flat bottom, straight sides,
a handle over.
I carried you in this.

A few months old,
you lay in this,
looked straight up at me
from below my hand,
your eyes yet blue.

Tucked in there,
you seemed to enjoy
the swaying of it,
gripped by my right hand.
I felt you safe in this.

Today I gave it to the thrift shop.
You turned fifty this year.

The Apron

She calls,
quite rare now,
but lovely when she does.
Her voice,
so grown up,
news of passing
her driver's test.
It was Thanksgiving
I saw her last.

She's been cooking, she says,
a thing she loves to do.
It's in her blood,
her mother's side,
the Mediterranean custom
of cinnamon with meat,
and olive oil with everything.
And baking too,
her fancy tarts,
her cakes.

And "Nana," she says,
"you were going to
sew me an apron."
My heart leaps!
Had I forgotten?

"Of course," I say, "Of course,
and how should we design it?"
"Nana, that's up to you,"
she says, "and now I've got to go."

A deep breath,
a wide smile,
and I'm off to my cupboards
to ponder through my fabrics.
Cottons, woolens, silks,
blues and purples, oranges and yellows.
What would please her most?
I see her, flour to her elbows,
laughing, tasting.
On the bottom shelf,
at the bottom of the pile,
I find it, an instant decision.
Red poppies, white daisies,
blue hyacinths, spread wild across
a sea of sweet blue grey.
This fabric has seen life
once before, the skirt of
my mother's sundress, worn
for picnics with my dad and me.

Sixty years I travel back
and feel the crisp cotton
on my mother's outstretched legs,
her toes dabbling in
the twinkling current of the Duddon.
My dad's tie flaps in the wind.
I am wearing Clark's sandals
with the flower pattern cut-out
on the toes.

I take out my tape measure
and, yes, there is enough.
I imagine it, the apron top pressed
against my granddaughter's chest,
the loop around her neck.
I'll join in another wild fabric
to give it ties around her waist.
I can see her smiling.

My scissors clip,
my machine hums.
Though I will press on,
I will not hurry this.

On the Hill

The night became intimate like a little plaza.
—Federico Garcia Lorcas

The night becomes intimate,
like a little plaza,
the minute it drops upon us.
Here, behind the house, the usual gang,
that satisfied feeling
after a rowdy round of bocce,
we gather close now on makeshift seats
around the settling fire.

Silence for a minute,
offers of fill-ups, glasses tinkling,
feet outstretched to the heat.
The stars join us,
not crowding in,
just carrying on their own conversations.
A breeze whistles the trees,
enough to keep the bugs at bay.

We know we have a feast to share.
Inside, the table is already laden.
But for now we linger,
thankful for all we have here
together on the hill.

II: Far

At Istanbul Airport

The women's bathroom at Istanbul airport
could be any other in the world.
Toilets flush,
stall doors bang,
women in all colors
flash across the mirrors on the walls.

In the bustle,
three girls emerge
to wash their hands and primp.
The youngest, maybe ten,
in skinny jeans and T-shirt,
checks the look of her shining hair,
her face excited,
gleeful, pretty.

Were they her sisters with her,
perhaps thirteen and fourteen,
flashing lovely eyes in the mirror too,
brimful with exuberance?
I couldn't tell for sure,
couldn't see their smiles
behind the black cloth
over their noses and mouths,
couldn't see the pretty jut of their chins,
the gleaming of their hair
under the black veils,
couldn't see their slim waists
under their black robes
to the floor.

Together they bounced out the door,
off on a plane to who knows where,
one lovely skinny girl,
and two small black ghosts,
giggling as all girls do.

Karacaagac

I

At the end of the day, they gave us flowers,
the children calling their loud goodbyes.
Full of village cooking, we climbed onto the bus,
sped out of their lives, so briefly known.

On the road again, we smiled at the happy chaos
of that schoolyard, the crush of the schoolroom,
the children's voices competing in welcome.
We savored the intimacy of the home kitchen,
eating together at the long table,
the many dishes prepared since early morning,
the mousaka, the minted yogurt sauce,
the small roasted potatoes.
We pondered the halting, the patience
of conversation in translation,
the talk of grandchildren, weddings,
such things in common.

And now we sped deeper into their country,
their power lines and their olive trees stretching
as far as our eyes could see.

II

Five tables under a canopy of vines,
the men playing their hands at cards,
their sweet smoke climbing, no breeze.

Perhaps one eyebrow rises
as we enter sheepishly, an interruption.
Inside we draw to one table,
Turkish tea, yes, all of us except for one,
a small glass bottle of Coke,
like a memory,
the old size that used to be enough.

Our language clatters,
an alien tongue.
They bide their time,
and we are gone.

The Taj Across the River

The crows fill the trees.
Small Indian crows, their voices
chorus the air of the Taj Mahal,
hundreds of them, tribal.

The trees wear painted white shoes.
Some trees are cropped short, no crows.
Everywhere pink stone,
except the Taj, pearly as old white socks.

From across the water the sound of a hammer
repairing a boat. Ducks float. Skinny girls
with switches herd their goats along the river shore.
Following them a pariah dog, his tail a flag.
A tiny girl carries fuel wood on her head.
Women follow her with great bundles
of green cattle feed.

The thin bleat of goats against the setting sun.
Smoke from a cooking fire rises undecidedly.
The Taj wears the worn lace of prim undergarments,
white linen bound up in symmetry.
Four light houses at her four corners, beamless.

At the Carpet Factory

Her small body
crimped over her loom,
her small hands
fly into knots,
a long-skilled blur.

Turquoise orange deep blue,
silk threads line up
tightly at her bidding,
beaten into density

How slowly her work climbs,
centimeter by centimeter,
week by week.
The pile of her work
brings me to my knees,
dazzled.

Varanasi

The full moon is at our backs
low in the darkening sky.
In our boat we are hushed,
rocked as our boat rocks,
rocked in a hundred small boats,
rocked by Mother Ganga,
on the river all together,
rocked, rocked, and blessed.

Across the broad ghats,
sparks mix with light,
light splashes in the dark water,
water reflects back to us
the red and gold of crackling fires,
fires for the burning of bodies,
bodies carried for miles on roof racks,
on carts, on strong shoulders,
to burn in this holy place.

The chanting of the priests rises,
drums throbbing, moonlight dancing
on the jewels in their turbans,
their tunics, their slippers, their feet flashing.
Branches punctuate the backlight,
ten pyres ready for the lucky bodies
to receive their deepest wishes.
Stripped now of their cloth of gold thread, red silk,
waiting now in simple white winding sheets,
they settle humbly on the careful pyres.

Is it a son, a brother,
a father who throws the first flame?
Smoke rises in ten tall columns.
The coals glow bright in the moonlit air,

snap fountains of sparks,
illuminate the gathered faces,
faces turned upward in joy and duty.

How long does a body burn?
When does a bone loosen from its joints
and fall to the ashes below?
When does a skull explode into fireworks?

The boys of the ghat poke at the coals
with long poles, poke to ensure the burning
is complete, leave nothing more for the flames.
They gather small piles of half-burned wood
to take home to their own hearths.

Rajasthan

On this cinnamon ground,
parched shrubs wait for monsoon rains.
No clouds, the sky is blued into haze.
So many birds make unfamiliar sounds,
have unfamiliar names.
Who are these skinny dogs,
thin dugs parched and gnawed?
Who are these skinny girls, bright as
butterflies, tugging at heartstrings for cash?

Then a man with a smile.
Do I want to buy a goat?
The breeze sighs.
"No goat on bus" he seems to understand.

Close to the ground, a tiny purple flower.
I reach for it—for what?
For another thing for me?
Its hidden thorns punish me,
remind me of my place.

Women gather fuel under the acacias,
small dry branches fallen since yesterday.
"Hey, money for me, how about that?"
They hack at twigs to feed their cook fires.
Their words, sharp as their little scythes,
slash at this stranger's heart.

The herder slowly passes with his black goats,
the few green shoots devoured without a chance.

III: Them

Concert

The cheering, the clapping, the yelling of bravos
softens into the lingering warmth of the auditorium.
Then the shuffling of feet, the squeaking of seats,
the low-toned calls of goodnight,
as she lingers in her seat as long as she can.
She rises to her feet at last, sways as she rises, reaches
back for her worn coat, pulls on her old misshapen hat,
feels for the small sandwich still concealed in her pocket.
Not too fast, she thinks, balance carefully,
just make it to the lobby, just make it to the street.
And her footsteps are steady now, out to the sidewalk,
disappearing beneath the underpass,
melting into its shadows, hidden from the cold moon.
And as she eases her bones gently down
into her pile of damp blankets, her heart
still soars in flight with the violins,
sings with the cello, dances with the flute.
Soon, with a tired smile, she sleeps.

Sunny Acres

Old trailer homes rock in the wind.
Catch the whiff of sewage again,
no cash to fix that tank.
Skinny dogs on chains
threaten warily,
damp leaves scattering.
Trash barrels, bungied in
the back of a pick-up,
wait for the clandestine
haul along the old train tracks
to the sluggish river bank.
Plastic flowers in
plastic pots attempt
some color.
Trailing an armless Barbie,
a small girl greets me
with a smile.

Bad Off

Here, this must be the place, right in here,
damn it, could've missed it.
Guess there's a reason it's not easy to find.
They told me behind Hannaford's,
but this is just a muddy track and a field.
I'm going slow here, might've got it wrong.
Christ, watch out for these ruts now, greasy too.
Wonder who'll be here, who else is so bad off.

I've been parking at Walmart,
they used to be good about that,
campers and stuff, stay in the back row,
maybe use the bathroom at Burger King.
But that's all stopped now, I panicked at first.
The food shelf people at that new Baptist church,
the pink-painted one where they mess with guitars,
they were the ones told me about this place.
Well, here it is.

Aye, seems quiet enough. Maybe I'll be all right here.
But, oh, no, look at that, there's lots more vehicles!
More over there under them trees!
Christ, it's a whole damn town!
I was hoping for something quiet, place to myself maybe,
hell with that, I guess.
Well, maybe I'll stop just a few nights,
try to get some rest.

No, Christ, look over there, there's even kids!
No, I hadn't reckoned on that!
Christ, not sure I can deal with that.
Well, just for tonight maybe,
pull up there at the end of that far row,

turn off this damned engine, breathe.
I'll climb in the back for a while,
pull those old blankets up, disappear.
Hope I can sleep. Maybe I'll dream.
My old farm. My dogs.

PTSD

He wears a gun charm,
probes its cylinder skyward,
his badges rescued from the forest floor.

Father, Father, I whisper,
please do not return
to Afghanistan.

Fleeting, he kodaks the shuttlecock,
camera obscura, nailed down
like a kid did it, playful.

Or desperate.
I beg him not to join the battle,
knowing full well he will.

I listen to his last music,
and he draws me in.
Is this his revenge?

As perfection in miniature,
he hides in his box,
disguised as five strings.

I stop and listen.
Is there a part for me here?
I see him hand over his trust,

a wind-up job, sign of the patriots,
a music box to mechanize his heart.
I see him salute, raise his helmet to the sky.

But I know he cannot hear me, the embroidered
emblems over his ears. How can I know
if he's for real, hanging here by a thread?

I hold my breath as he deftly
avoids a fly paper sent to him
as a death trap. Flit, flit.

A luggage label will only take you so far,
show you the whole world
in bright colors.

Quiet his heart. Toss him in the air
like a beach ball, this is a big boy's game.
But wait, is this the wrong battle?

Get serious. Get ready for the big heavy.
Is this party magician always so casual?
Over paid, over easy?

Here's the chance for him to escape, now before
the tears all dissolve. This is key.
But then they come,

the ones he's been waiting for,
his throw-away people, holding together now,
singing in the murky streets, singing for their lives.

We meet face to face at last.
Father, didn't I know you once?
What did you tell me?

Thank You for Your Service

You bundle up your bedding from the sidewalk,
straps trailing, pillows falling.
Your eyes are lost to another world
of stillness, where water ripples.

You clutch to yourself your ragged coat,
stooping, frail as a clothes tree.
Rain drops like fairy lights
scatter on your close-cropped head,
twinkle in the damp electric air.
You straighten up and load your back.
You breathe, and soften.

Then sirens scald the air.
You wince to the bone.
Eyes wide now, you face Fallujah,
reach into your coat and feel
for your rusted weapons,
fire your imaginary bullets into
the foggy yellow air.

To Take the Dead Weight

To take the dead weight
Of the knee on his neck
For the shape of his lips
For the shade of his skin

The knee on his neck
For the width of his nose
For the shade of his skin
For the words in his voice

Not even a bullet
For the shape of his lips
For the words in his voice
For the width of his nose

His face in the dirt
For the shape of his lips
The knee on his neck
To take the dead weight

IV: Other

Border

No shoes, just bleeding feet,
rock scarred in the dust.
No stars tonight,
just clouds, a milky darkness.

Rock scarred in the dust,
one step then the next.
Just clouds, a milky darkness,
a hundred figures moving.

One step then the next,
shoulders stooped with burden.
A hundred figures moving,
fathers, mothers, children.

Shoulders stooped with burden,
bundled infants, water,
fathers, mothers, children.
Coyotes trot alongside.

Bundled infants, water.
No stars tonight.
Coyotes trot alongside.
No shoes, just bleeding feet.

Invasion

"Let them eat cake," she said,
her white-gloved hands preening,
her nose raised, her eyebrows.

"Theirs is the hand they were dealt,
so be it. Don't trouble me now,
I have days to fill with pleasures.
Bring me my succulents."

And was it not ever thus.
"Put their children in cages,
the silly fools for coming.

"Let them eat flies. A pound
of flies contains more protein
than a pound of beef."

This I Pray

That these skinny mules will keep their pace
at least 'til dusk, swallowing up
these kilometers unchallenged.

That my mother's licorice eyes will never again
be stung by these poisoned sands.

That we will lift our heads and open our mouths to rain.
That my children will know oranges, peaches, grapes.

That my loom will be unbroken, and once more
I will shuttle the heavy wool from my own sheep,
felt it densely and keep my children dry.

That I will dip my hands deep in flour,
once again forming the loaves of life.

Plight

Afterwards, they told us it was
because we weren't the ones they wanted.
Cast-offs, they called us,
drifters around the edges of the world,
fed occasionally by nuns.
Grief was our common fare,
and humbly we digested it.
It never occurred to us to
juxtapose our lot with theirs,
kneeling in their dirt.
Mud was our bed sheet,
noxious weeds our pillow.
Over and over, one of us would
pass on without a word.
Questions were not our currency.
Rung after rung, we climbed their cliffs,
strangled by the frayed ropes of their disgust.
They did not notice.
Unleashed into the vacuous night,
we sought out their poison supper pits
named for Xavier the Archangel.
Yellow as piss, we sucked it in.
Zeitgeist. They had us forever.

Why I Stole His Lamp

Because he is rich and can buy another in the blink of an eye,
peeling bills from his wallet like my mother peels onions.

Because it is in the nighttime that he digs his tunnel.
Already it reaches under the doghouse near the border.

Because his tunnel will bring us danger.
Because he is known to break promises.

Because he refuses to guide the children, refuses to
light their way to the supplies of water.

Because with a lamp we may guide the children, show them
the potholes and the pitfalls, bring them safely over.

Because the moon is not enough.

Another Color

> *Maybe they will be another color*
> *That no-one has ever seen before.*
> —Jo Harjo

Maybe they'll be other colors that no-one has ever seen before.
Maybe they're among us already but we've been too blind to see.
Their beauty is not our beauty and we do not see it.
We cannot hear their music because it is not our music.
We cannot make words of their words because they are not our
  words.
Their stories are not our stories and we cannot listen.

They may come to us not in need but in curiosity.
They offer gifts but we dismiss them as insignificant.
They are persistent and full of kindness.
They believe in us, believe that deep in us
there must be remnant beauty.
But this is not our story.
This is not the story we tell our children.
This is not the reflection we see in our waters.
In sadness they turn away
and are gone.

V: Outside

At Zero

at zero degrees
eight blue jays
commanding the perches
hungry as sin

eight blue jays
poking at chickadees
hungry as sin
bossing the woodpeckers

poking at chickadees
seeds spilling over
bossing the woodpeckers
ground seed for doves

seeds spilling over
snow spray from branches
ground seed for doves
flapping and jabbing

snow spray from branches
commanding the perches
flapping and jabbing
at zero degrees

Field Notes from Jane's Farm, Kirkby Lonsdale

Lichen me to a cold spring, sheep baaing
Stick to a stone, star-shaped, no grazing
Flood pool, cracked like a puzzle
One dock, soothe my nettle

Wire barb, crows, wind blade
Hawthorn, holly, hedge laid
Mole piles hoof pocked
Iron trough brimming

Along the Edge

Just give me rime
Along the edge
No rima pudendi
Just hoar this day

Along the edge
Thick hoar this morning
Just hoar this day
A soft white coat

Thick hoar this morning
Chillest yet
A soft white coat
No rilles no craters

Chillest yet
Wrap up wrap up
No rilles no craters
No glottis vera

Wrap up wrap up
No rima pudendi
No glottis vera
Just give me rime

Trick of the Light

It is two on a February afternoon
at 44 latitude. The sun,
single-minded in its descent,
feels a pull toward true west.

Imbolc, at the cross quarter day,
is behind us. Already we are
hurtling toward
the equinox.

As human creatures,
are we hefted on light
as we are hefted on the familiar
ground that raised us?
In exile, at an alien latitude,
do I spend a continuum of days,
sunrise after sunset,
in futile attempt to adjust
to a quantity of sunlight
that jars with the light in my eyes?

In these yet dark, shortest days,
I kindle my need fires
and keep the dark outside my doors.
Every dawn I listen intently
for the bird chatter that signals daylight.
Every evening I light candles at my shrines,
baiting the dark to disappear.
The wind sneaks inside
through cracks in the door,
makes the vulnerable candles flutter.
I keep faith and wait.

April

This so-called spring
brought out new guns
to test me,
sleet reinforcements and ruts
so deep my axles
choked and faltered,
christ, will I ever reach home?
Over and over I wish
I had the attitude,
the necessary chin
that real Vermonters
show, dismissive of
people like me,
soft people who don't
have what it takes,
don't measure up,
fall down.
And the bear comes
to the suet in the nighttime
and my wary cat
runs high up
the tree in the dawn.
And the town truck
throws five more loads of gravel
into our hill
as I gaze out and pray
for deliverance.

After Harvesting Ramps in the Vermont Woods in Early May

Convince me.
Was it always like this?
Did the water lap the bottom
step in springtime?
Did the birds return
as the magnolia burst into blossom?
Or did the people bow to hunger
well into June and, even then,
wrench at the churning in their guts,
filled up on ramps and dandelions?
Or were there bright new shoots
we've never heard of,
green blades rising from the snow banks,
deep roots to roast in shimmering coals?
Might there be one last April rooster
to mount on the spit
and turn, turn, in the pale sunshine,
juices dripping into a wide, flat pan
of unleavened bread?
Might there even be a bridegroom
and a bride, choked
by a winter of desire, emerging now,
relieved and awkward,
bowing deeply to each other,
promising fertility
again and again?

No. You shan't deceive me.
These were the stories they
told each other. Fool's gold.
The winter ruled longer than

anyone dared tell.
Warmth was but a legend
told to small children,
their skin deep cracked with cold.
No woman wore the bridal bonnet.
No man dared dream of touch.

Nasturtiums

Were I but one of these
green fire in the mouth
hot stuff in the salad
surprise the guests

but who came along
bit off
all your profuse first leaves
bushing out in competition
for rain
for light
for the sheer fun of it?

and now though
see how you
made it an opportunity
stayed short and
burst into flower
my favorite orange yellow
those too so hot
on the tongue
Were I but one of these

This I Pray

That the fierce clatter of rain
will cease,
and the giddy wind will tire
of making waves.

That the sly waters of the lake
will once more sidle up to
the reaching of the rushes,
lapping, lapping,
rebuilding the shoreline from memory.

That bubbles will rise again
from the inky depths
as the breath of trout stirring
from reluctant sleep,
that their scales will flash as
rainbows in the timid sunlight
as they dare to leap for gnats
yet barely hatched.

That the earthworms will begin
their work anew,
their rosy bodies pushing, pushing
through the dark soil,
their five hearts steady,
working amongst the ancient roots of trees.

That with neither gullibility nor guile
we will rise from the water's chill
and begin again.

Cloud Speaks

I wandered lonely as a cloud that
floats on high o'er vales and hills.
          —William Wordsworth

You say you wandered.
You say I'm lonely and you wandered like me.
High up here, floating.
Like you think you know me.

I am droplets.
I am fluff.
I am aerosol.
I am veils, wisps, bands, ripples.
I am elephant, rowboat, tow truck, dog.
I am stratus, cirrus, cumulus.
I am stratiform veils,
cirriform wisps
stratocumuliform bands and ripples.

Do not claim to know me.
I do not know loneliness.
I am cloud.

Sky Furniture

Is it a full moon tonight?
Daylight yet, grey in a still-blue sky,
a round moon, disc moon,
fat cushion for resting Vs of geese,
a sunlit window into the cosmos.

But how soon full slides into wane,
wide becomes narrow.
Renewed, the new moon slips
from behind the clouds,
confident in its fresh, slim grace.

And how that sparkling hook
suggests a chair!
Have we not all seen it
in our storybooks, the elf,
the cheeky sprite with perky cap
who perches on that bright-lit hook?
Such a place to sit and sing,
plying the sky, dodging every cloud.

Sky furniture.
Well lit.

Fell Dreams

The first time I heard the bells, I was returning from a visit with Maribel. I had baked jam tarts for her, and, in return, she had plied me with fleece from her flock of Herdwicks hefted on the fell above her farm. The bells, seeming softly close and true, tinkled between each of my walking breaths, in and out, taking me happily home.

Just before sleeping, I heard the bells again. My bed was hard, too narrow for comfort, and the bells, a sound between air and water, soothed my body into dreaming, taking me up onto the fells to gather tufts of fleece from the wires that kept the sheep from the ravine. Between notes in the bells' song, I heard the sheep rustling in the brown-gold bracken.

Just before waking, I heard the bells grow louder and closer. Four young tups approached, heralding a noble ram. Fourteen sturdy ewes followed close behind. As the ram shook his curving horns, the sound of the bells reached a glorious crescendo. It was then I knew I would spin the fleece into the finest yarn, color it with lichens into purple, and bring the utmost pleasure to Maribel's sweet face.

Geese

That V,
that raucous, honking V,
that skein scraping across the spring blue sky,
northwards, northwards.
Who is that leader in the front,
their pace-setter, the bravest one that
takes the brunt, the guide?

But no, there's not just one.
Geese do not fight for power, for influence.
In turns they take it, replacing their front position
as each leader tires, the ones behind
honking in encouragement.
When the wind is strong, more frequently they share.

North by the sun to the east or west,
then by the stars at night.
Rivers too, long known, now taught to goslings.
Each bird aware of stragglers,
reaching out to rescue, catch up.
Each goose's wing providing uplift for those behind,
a rotating vortex of air.

No reins on this invisible chariot.
Just purpose, seeking fodder
in the summer north, the winter south.
Grains, grasses, roots, shoots, greens under water,
they eat for half a day, then sleep head under wing
'til the skies envelop them again.

Wild geese, what lessons do you have for me?
Shall I learn your geometric principles of flight,
sing in roisterous chorus,

write my poems with your quills?
Better surely to honor your Anatidaean arrangements,
hallow your fields and marshes,
learn to fly with grace and kindness.

Trees

Look, that wind
through those far
trees, see how their
leaves all turn their
backs on me,
show me their
pale undersides.

They know I'm
not a tree. I don't
buffet and flex
in the wind. I dare
not lose my coat
and face the winter
bare.

Sometimes it has to
be written across
the forest, written on
every tree, so you can
notice, so you can
come to your
senses and be
what you are.

Sometimes it takes
a great wind to
reveal the obvious,
to clear enough
space inside
your mind to
let the truth in.

Sometimes it's in
the remnants of trees,
blackened sticks
in the morning ashes,
that you find
a direction, a sign
pointing your
way on.

VI: Soon

Granddaughter

She texted me this morning,
said they'd come in second,
the pride somehow shining
from the short words on my screen.
Fifteen now, and rowing is her passion,
a team of eight in a boat,
straining, pulling hardest,
striving for the prize.

And the water sprays wide
in the hot New York sun,
mysteriously warm in April,
and their rosy faces glisten
sweet with sweat. One comments
how the water is already low,
one dares another for a dip.

I scan the years beyond her.
How early will the ice be out
when she is twenty-five?
How many mighty storms
will she withstand, a refugee crouched
on a mountain top, all possessions lost
on the drowned streets she fled?
How many farmers can feed her no bread?
Where will be a shack that might
still offer her shelter?

Unnoticed

It is 6 am on a Thursday in January.
Upstairs a man is bellowing in his sleep.
He speaks of resilience and how the local messiahs
must preach to the village.

In the kitchen the loaded stove
rumbles its teeth into three more logs of maple.
Outside it is ten degrees above zero.
The chill penetrates the loose window where

a woman sits in her place on the worn orange love seat.
She scrapes frost from the glass with a letter opener
her mother bought in Blankenberghe before she was born.
On it is painted a tiny ship and two seagulls.

Below in the valley grind endless trucks of consumer desires.
Pay Pal. Visa. Mastercard.
The mighty Amazon flows north,

spewing the struggling bodies of the last blue dolphins,
wriggling piranha the woman once visited
and caught for supper.

Unnoticed, the sea rises.
The clouds split into frost to keep her in the mountains,
scraping icy paths, shaking ashes to the ground
to guard against that one fatal slip.

Refuge

Between 7am and 8am,
the hours when the old people shop,
the man from Brooklyn walks his dog.
He is a stranger in this village,
unaccustomed to the gurgle of the river,
the steady hiss of the wind in the trees.

He watches with puzzled eyes
the quiet people, few now,
who walk briskly from small vehicles
to the stoop of the market store
to pick up pre-ordered groceries.
His dog watches their dogs in the car windows,
aching to play on the empty village green.

The man casts his eyes toward the water.
Branches loosed by the thaw
hurriedly float down the river of isolation.
Frost heaves wait to be soothed.
Leaves left to rot in the fall yearn now to be raked.

The man coughs and wonders.
He attempts to feel grateful for his refuge.
He has heard that the people in China
can now see the stars again.
One often finds life under dead stones.

Jane's Farm, Cumbria, 2019

Accept the invitation to walk
the narrow road, no room to pass.
Accept gladly the offer, be
ready for the start.
Know, however, to proceed with caution.
Know the pitfalls, know the temptations.
Know that you might never return.

On the side of the road you will notice
a dead jacket, leaking polyester.
You will mistake it for a sheep.
Stick to your senses.

On each side of the road, the bracken
will have been given a short haircut.
Short back and sides.
The ends of its stems will be sharp and sallow.
Pay attention.

You will delight in encountering
a great swath of willows,
their gold dancing with their green.
How tall they grow, how thick!
Were they always here?
What is their history?
Did they willingly submit to their subjugation,
the way they are bound together now into fences?
Who taught them this?
Did they not resist?

To the right now you will see half a tree,

like half a loaf, sliced down the middle.
It is a holly tree.
See its spiky leaves, teeth bared.
It might occur to you that such a tree
could stand a chance at fighting back,
press its teeth into the flesh of
progress bent on making way
for vehicles of metal.
I am told that long ago the holly did resist.
It failed and was wrenched out at the root.

Look now into the distance.
How tempting it is to keep on walking,
seeking a place unshattered,
a place unmolded,
a place not bent into submission.

No. Such a place exists only in rumours.
You are here now.
Instead, find joy in what is left.
Instead, breathe slowly,
feel this new, obliging beauty.

When We Are Gone

When we are gone,
there will still be a kettle of hawks
racing across the summer sky.

There will still be sleek, sparkling fish
waltzing in the shallows,
a parliament of owls still keeping watch
high in the branches of the oaks.

When we are gone,
clouds will still form and reform,
shape themselves into boxes, and busses,
cathedrals, lions, and dogs.

Committees of raccoons will still
raid the nests of guileless birds.
Coffles of dusty donkeys will still seek shade
beneath the creaking branches of old trees.

When we are gone,
when our last remains are tossed into the sea,
this world may reassemble,
this time in favor of
fur and feather, carapace and scales.

All creatures that survive now
in pain, decline, enslavement,
may surge again to take their rightful turn
on this green orb in space.

To My Great-Granddaughter Not Yet Born

There used to be these things called birds.
No, they weren't insects.
They'd fly around all the time, but
no, they weren't insects.
Most of them were about the size of your hand
but some were a lot bigger.
Some were really small.
Some of them sang beautiful songs.

Birds were covered with things called feathers,
long spines with soft fine hair on them.
The spines came out of their skins
and all the hairs of the feathers lay flat.
The feathers might be grey or black
but lots of them had red in them
or white or blue or yellow.
The feathers on their wings were long
and that's what made them fly.
Some of them would fly thousands of miles
to look for summer.
Some of them stayed around all winter in the snow.
I wish you could have seen them.

VII: Late

Born

> *Being human is a guest house.*
> —Rumi

What sort of thing is a life?
This thing sourced at the whim or plea
of two other lives soon gone,
trundled along pathways undesigned,
tricked into purpose.

What sort of scaffold can a life climb
to look back, to look forward,
to change course, to defy
the promise of importance?
What chance is there to
wink and turn about?

This life will not be gift-wrapped.
Not leached of color,
not offered finally as a cup of dust.
This life will be a wild chant,
sung by a psalm singer in the lion house.
This life will wield a pen racing to
keep up with a mercurial mind.

The rest may be silence.

By the Side of the Road

I just saw Adonis.
If I'd been driving any faster I'd have missed him.
There, round the bend, on the side of our road,
and I waved because
at first I thought it was
the nice guy who lives there.
But no!
Oh, this was something special!
Shirt off, that bare chest such a pretty color,
those slim hips hardly holding up his jeans,
him planting bushes.
And he waved back at me, of course,
like we all do on our road,
slightly puzzled that it seemed I knew him.
Oh, did I smile!
Me, could've been his grandma,
lapping him up like there was
no tomorrow.

Off Ramp

What is the past tense of loss?
Will profit return,
obliterate memory?

Will I be holy at a loss,
regretting what I squandered,
small flowers trampled underfoot,
life's overdraft whistling through the trees?

Is this a disappearing act,
a plethora of punctuation?
An invisible ebb,
a silent toll unnoticed?
Not yet, not yet.

What then is my undoing?
No mischief, no fall from grace.
No witnesses.
Just an expiration date,
shelf life clearly printed.
A frost over everything.

Enough

They say that if
I put these stones in my mouth
and jangle them around
in my sturdy old-age teeth
I will be given the privilege of
one extra day of life
The trick is deciding whether
it's worth the bother

True, the stones are smooth
rounded at their corners by
years in the sand, the tide
coming and going
coming and going
Two of the stones are white and one is grey
I have them here
in the palm of my hand
kidnapped from a secret place by the sea

I ponder
Just one day?
Perhaps one day with bleeding gums
sharp edges of chipped teeth
against my still-plump tongue?

No, I say
Firmly no
I will return now to that shore
let the waves wash my feet
deliver these blameless stones
back to the sand

Catastrophic

My cat is eating the obituaries.
The cold outdoors drives him
to indoor sport, to flirt
with the newspaper, to pounce
on its wafting page and chew it.
He fades the names of the dead
in a blur of ink and grime.
With a casual swat, he tears
apart the lists of the grieving,
the petty accomplishments
writ large, the pleas
for remembrance.

I see my own name under his paws.
Is the paragraph long
or short?
Do my sons embellish me
or keep me brief?
My eyes shift top left
to read the date.
It's already chewed,
an illegible blur.

About the Author

Ina Anderson was born and raised in Cumbria in the northwest of England. She has now lived in Vermont for many years. Her first work was in editing scientific journals, including the *Journal of Neurosurgery,* and *Icarus: International Journal of Solar System Science,* with editor Carl Sagan. She later took to teaching, spending over twenty years at the Community College of Vermont as a faculty member and student advisor, teaching writing, speaking, and literature. Ina's poems have appeared in many publications, including *Birchsong, This Place I Know, When All This Is Over, The Mountain Troubadour, Poem Town Randolph,* and *Literary North.* Several of her poems appeared in the Pie Poets anthologies, *Perhaps It Was the Pie,* 2014, and *The Party Cabinet,* 2023. Her first collection, *Journey into Space,* published in 2017 by Antrim House, was nominated for a Pushcart Prize.

www.ingramcontent.com/pod-product-compliance
Lightning Source LLC
Chambersburg PA
CBHW071010160426
43193CB00012B/1996